At Bat II

At Bat II

Poems by

Mel Glenn

© 2023 Mel Glenn. All rights reserved.
This material may not be reproduced in any form, published,
reprinted, recorded, performed, broadcast,
rewritten or redistributed without
the explicit permission of Mel Glenn.
All such actions are strictly prohibited by law.

Cover design by Shay Culligan
Cover photo by Adam Vilimek

ISBN: 978-1-63980-348-4

Kelsay Books
502 South 1040 East, A-119
American Fork, Utah 84003
Kelsaybooks.com

For my new grandson, Casey,
May he grow up happy, healthy,
and a New York Mets fan

Contents

Introduction

The Back Pages	13
Spring Training	14
The First Game	15

The Poems

A European Looks at Baseball	19
A Long Season	20
Baseball Averages Saved Me	21
Baseball, Like Chess	22
Big Data at the Ball Park	23
Can't Wait	24
Cheating	25
Childhood Games	26
Dissection of a Game	27
Extra Innings—A Proposal	28
Fair Is Foul	29
Grapefruit League	30
Gun Day at the Ball Park	31
Happy Felton's Knot Hole Gang	32
I Am Not Myself	33
I Am Suing My Knees	34
I Need a Hero	35
Is Baseball Dying?	36
Karl Spooner—Who?	37
Missing Part of My Life During Covid	38
Movie Quotes and Baseball	39
My Favorite Things	40
My First Baseman's Glove	41
Nobody Lives in K.C.	42
Nobody Remembers Punchball	43
No Joy in Mudville	44

On Seeing a Brooklyn Dodgers Baseball Cap	45
On Winning	46
Patsy's Pork Store	47
Pitchers and Catchers Report	48
Poetry in the Minor Leagues	49
Redemption, Baseball's Crowning Glory	50
Reply to Replays	51
Requiem for a Losing Ball Club	52
Sahr Amara	53
Sandlot Ball	54
Scouting Report	55
Second Place	56
Silly Names in Baseball #1	57
Silly Names in Baseball #2	58
Sports for the Masses	59
Street Games	60
Surely, He's Worth More	61
Teacher All-Star	62
Ten in a Row	63
The Almost No-Hitter and the Open Boat	64
The Antidote to Aging	65
The Batting Cage	66
The Body Shambles	67
The Closer	68
The Jewish Ballplayer	69
The Losing Pitcher Talks to His Therapist	70
The Mets Meet the Met	71
The Natural	72
They Don't Know Punchball	73
Time on Their Hands	74
Unwatchable	75
Walk-Off Home Run	76
We Need Our Heroes	77
When My Team Wins	78

White Man's Baseball	79
Wild Card	80
Winter Ball	81

Ending Poems

The Last Picture Show	85
Why We Cheer	86
Why Baseball Is Important	87

Introduction

The Back Pages

Sports shape us.
We grew up reading the newspapers
from the back pages to the front.
We studied box scores
as if they were religious texts.
We gave our heroes powers
we wish we had.
Who has not imagined
hitting a walk-off home run,
knocking in a 20-foot putt,
kicking the winning field goal?
We expect our sports to provide
the excitement our lives lack
as we work, toil and dream.
Sports exist as the link
between fathers and sons,
mothers and daughters.
We play together so we won't die alone.
We wish to make ourselves heroes
in our own eyes.
Let's play ball!

Spring Training

The field of my dreams sparkles in the morning sun
as players swat home runs like flies in batting cages,
while others in the outfield camp under arching trajectories,
flicking at the descending orbs with practiced grace.
Pot-belied coaches check their clipboards,
adjust their sunglasses, chew some gum,
waiting for the game and the season to begin.
I am hopeful for a successful start,
well before injuries start to mount.
I am seven years old now with my glove and bat,
nervous with excitement at the start of my life,
well before errors fill up my stat sheet.
Now the green fields roll out before me,
alive with singles, doubles, and triples.
The smells of spring training—a perfume to be
bottled and kept until the official first game begins.

The First Game

The first ball thrown
is the appearance of a new leaf.
The first ball caught
is the newly green expanse of the field.
The first game of the year
repudiates our seasonal ice age.
Time to shed winter coats
and don the catcher's chest protector.
Time to shed our mittens,
and break in our new first baseman's glove.
Instead of shoveling out my driveway,
I can rake the dirt between first and second.
Instead of slogging through snowdrifts,
I can once more fly around the bases.
My spirit soaring, I am the kid
playing sandlot ball, my winter replaced by
the first ball thrown, the first ball caught,
this ballet to be repeated until
the fading twilight of the fall.

The Poems

A European Looks at Baseball

My name is Matteo,
and I have lived my whole life
here in Zurich, Switzerland.
How then to look at baseball,
which I have seen on YouTube.
It is indeed a slow game
with most of the players
standing around for
much of the time,
unlike football when
the players and the ball
are always in motion.
Only at times is the baseball up in the air.
Also, why does one team stay in a trench,
allowing only one player out at a time?
Why, too, does a baseball game
go on for so long that people leave early?
In football, after 90 minutes, generally,
the game, it is finished.
In baseball, the players are
burdened with much equipment,
bats, masks and gloves,
but in football the players
are encouraged to run free.
Baseball is an odd game, no?
Football is the King of all Sports!

A Long Season

When I panic that my team
has lost two in a row, oh my,
my friend, Sam, counsels me.
"It's a long season," he says.
Indeed. Baseball plays on,
stretching its arms out
over a 162-game schedule.
What other sports season is
so languorously long?
The clock, the master
of most pro teams,
is not welcome here,
though initial attempts
have been made to limit
time on the pitching mound.
So, I will take a deep breath,
consult the calendar
instead of my watch, and
luxuriate in the warm bath of
a long and effervescent season.

Baseball Averages Saved Me

I am what I am—or was,
a near-sighted nerd
whose vision extended only to
the box scores in the daily papers.
Batting averages saved me,
the three-digit numbers
that tracked and certified
the fortunes of my favorite players.
I would make up dice games
with my teams, a precursor to
the popular fantasy baseball games today.
I was ever wary of venturing outside
to meet the neighborhood bullies
who delighted in my fearfulness.
So, with pale skin and bad eyes,
I took refuge in my room,
and hovered over my players,
calculating their hits and misses.
No, I did not become a statistician,
but survived the pubic wars,
knowing there was safety in numbers,
numbers carried out to the third place.

Baseball, Like Chess

In the winter months,
baseball, like chess,
moves its players
across the board
as executives from
major league teams
pitch and toss plans,
trying to capture pieces
from opposing sides.
Some players are pawns
to be sacrificed and traded.
They have little say where
and how they will be moved.
Other, more valuable pieces,
evaluate their direction
to seek a better position.
The goal is to catch valuable assets.
My team, the New York Mets,
just lost a valuable pitcher.
Will they now recoup, get new pieces,
and live to fight another game?
Have they devised a winning strategy?

Big Data at the Ball Park

There once was a time when
baseball was stunningly simple.
Wins, batting averages and RBIs
were all you needed to know.
Whether scout, fan, or player,
one is now required to consult
a field manual full of strange sounding statistics.
"Who's on first?" has been replaced by
a slash line, OPS, WHIP and a ceiling on
the number of pitches thrown.
Pitchers pitch to quadrants; batters hit to zones,
and decisions for future employment are made
by men with Master's degrees in business.
And let us not even begin to talk about
umpires calling New York for decisions.
Furthermore, you want them to be
artificial intelligence robots now?
Oh, poor batter, encumbered
by numbers too heavy to bear.
Oh, poor pitcher, weighted down
by concerns about their arm angles.
Return, please, to an earlier time and place
when baseball was pure, and was not
a game for which a spread sheet is needed.

Can't Wait

Basketball bores me.
Football frightens me.
Soccer stupefies me.
Golf gags me.
Lacrosse loses me.
Boxing baffles me.
Track tires me.

But with baseball
I evade the winter winds,
cozily sitting in my chair
scanning the sports pages
to see who got traded.
I become immersed in
fiction and non-fiction articles,
theorizing about the new season.
I am warm next to my hot stove
gathering scouting reports and data.
I will be ready for spring training,
and cannot wait for the first pitch.

Cheating

Of course, there is no cheating in baseball.
Who would ever think that?
Like there is no cheating in politics,
marriage, or any other human activity.
Who would cheat in baseball?
Who would steal the innocence
of a young fan forcing his eyes to open?
Baseball is a pure, sacrosanct sport,
played by heroes with 100% rectitude,
athletes who exemplify the best of
American ideals and sportsmanship.
Of course, the playing field is level,
a democratic milieu where
merit and skills are rewarded,
and honesty and integrity are valued.
Who would want to destroy our faith,
besmirch our allegiance to a sport
and/or team that gives us reason to cheer.
Cheating in baseball? No way.
Why are you lying to me?

Childhood Games

Listen, my children,
you will never know
the joys of childhood games.
You are much too busy
playing on your iPhone 47, whatever.
You have never heard of stickball,
punchball and stoopball, have you?
A pink ball called a "Spaldeen,"
was thrown against the stoop—
five points for a catch on a bounce,
10 points on the fly, and if the ball
hit the corner of the step, 100 points!
You are much too busy texting
inane messages to friends,
describing what you are doing
at this exact moment.
You have forfeited your childhood
upon the altar of easy access to non-news.
But I, dear children, have memories
of long summer twilights when
the most important job I had
was to track a small pink ball until
it landed softly in my innocent hands.

Dissection of a Game

The morning regulars took their regular seats,
as Stella, the waitress, looked over their worn faces,
and said, "The usual, gentlemen?"
They all nodded like bobble-head dolls,
and talked about last night's game.
"I would have taken him out after
he walked the first two batters in the 6th."
"I would have pinch-hit for Smith in the 7th."
"I wouldn't have used Diaz in the 8th.
He's pitched too many innings already."
They continued to nod like baseball bobble-head dolls.
Stella brought the oatmeal,
scrambled eggs and pancakes,
placing the separate dishes before each man
as she had done countless times before.
"Coffee later?" she asked, knowing, but being polite.
"Next year will be better," one man said, "you'll see."
They all nodded like baseball bobble-head dolls.

Extra Innings—A Proposal

Baseball, most certainly
lacks the speed of
basketball, football, and hockey,
or any other major sport,
with the exception of golf.
It remains true to its pastoral roots
with only twenty-two minutes of
ball-in-flight in a four-hour game.
Having emerged sleep-deprived
from a late, extra inning game,
I offer the following proposal:
If, after nine innings, the score is tied,
each team selects the batter due up
and whoever does better—
a hit trumps a strikeout,
a walk beats a groundball out—
that team is declared the winner.
If, let's say, both players strike out,
the next hitter in the lineup comes to bat.
The home team always has last licks.
Purists may raise objections
to my baseball sudden death,
but, frankly, I need my sleep.

Fair Is Foul

Shakespeare knew his baseball
and suggested there be
no distinction between
fair and foul balls.
Like with a cricket pitch,
all areas of the playing field
should be considered fair territory.
Baseball is slow; snails play faster,
so consider having all foul balls
in play, handled by fielders
scooping up grounders that ricochet
off the left or right railings or nets.
For foul balls that reach the stands,
the batter would be allowed
only two such shots, and would
be retired after a third such ball.
The baselines would be necessary
only for running.
This proposal should make
baseball more exciting and faster,
thus, pleasing the Bard and
millions of impatient fans.

Grapefruit League

"Hope is a thing with feathers,"
Emily Dickinson famously said.
I try to remember that
as I scan the box scores
of spring training games
wondering if each name
I don't recognize will blossom
into an all-star player.
Hope is a batter stepping up to the plate,
a pitcher beginning his wind-up,
a manager filling out his line-up card.
Hope is the next batter,
the next game, the next series.
It is this tenuous string to the heart
that keeps one alive.
It is the smile of a young kid
pounding his glove at third,
praying that the next ground ball
will be hit to him so he can make the play.
Hope is as large as a grapefruit
which may or may not be pulverized
as the season slips into summer.

Gun Day at the Ball Park

"Welcome to Gun Day at the ballpark, folks.
I'm your broadcaster 'Bazooka' Bill Murphy,
and here now is your starting line-up for
your Texas Rangers. First, we will be right back
after a word from our sponsor, the NRA."

"We're back - Leading off, 'Bullet' Bob Anderson, (ss)
Batting second, 'Shooter' Randy McCoy, (3rd)
Third up, Carl, 'the Rifleman' Cox, (rf)
Cleanup, 'Pistol' Paul Snyder, (cf)
Batting 5th, Henry 'the Tank' Williams, (1b)
Batting 6th, Jerry Glock, (2nd)
Batting 7th, Fuzzy Remington, (c)
Batting 8th, Colt Bandolier (lf)
and the DH, batting 9th, B.B. Arsenal
and warming up in the bullpen is A.R. Winchester

Today is 'Have Gun, Will Travel' Day at the park.
Will you now please rise, cross your guns over your heart,
while we play our national anthem, 'I Shot the Sheriff.'"

Happy Felton's Knot Hole Gang

So what if my European father
never played catch with me.
So what if I cried like a baby
when Kevin Costner had a catch
with his father in "Field of Dreams."
I had my own dreams with Happy Felton
who ran a televised kid's show before
every home game of my beloved Brooklyn Dodgers.
Three youngsters would run, throw and field
while some larger-than-life Dodger hero
would judge the best 10-year-old athlete.
I was that kid fielding a ground ball,
angling under a pop-up and throwing
a major league hardball as fast as I could.
In my reverie, I always won and Happy,
smiling, would ask me my name, my face
broadcast over the whole tri-state area.
Sometimes, I think of Happy now
as I toss a baseball from hand to hand,
and think of the times when my only wish
was to star in Happy Felton's Knot Hole Gang program.

I Am Not Myself

I am not myself these days.
I am 23, trying to make it to the Bigs.
    I am 79, trying to make it to the bathroom.
I take my glove and run out onto the field.
    I take my lunch and go sit in the park.
I toss the ball to the second baseman.
    I toss breadcrumbs to the pigeons.
I check my stance in the batter's box.
    I check to see if I still have my keys.
I take ground balls in the infield.
    I take my medications.
I feel the hot, bright Florida sun.
    I feel it's going to rain soon.
I tap the dirt off my spikes with my bat.
    I click my cane as I trudge back home.

I am not myself for six glorious weeks.
I am every hopeful kid in spring training,
dreaming of playing major league ball.
I am not myself these days.

I Am Suing My Knees

I am suing my knees—
for non-support.
Things fall apart,
and my poor knees
have decided to disassemble first.
Can anything be done
to hold up their structural integrity,
short of replacing them
in some fearful medical procedure?
Maybe I can shore up their defense
with a brace or two, or bring
some relevant medicine to bear,
anything to forestall the attack of the
torn meniscus and rampant arthritis.
My knees besiege me, weakening my will
and slowing my pace to a turtle's crawl.
Stairs, you make me reel in pain.
I'd gladly trade my knees for a new pair,
for which I'll pay you next Tuesday.
My knees are bringing me to my knees.
How do ballplayers cope with their injuries?

I Need a Hero

My favorite ballplayer has just
struck out on three pitches
in the top of the ninth with
the tying and go-ahead runs on base.
Ball game over. Put it in the books!
I don't ask for a Joe DiMaggio.
I don't care where he's gone.
I don't need a Greek god or five-tool player.
I only want a modest hero, someone
reliable who can hit .300,
who can produce an occasional home run,
who can play his position with confidence.
Million-dollar salaries—for what?
Daily highlight reel accomplishments—
who needs 'em?
Maybe I would just settle for
a player who shows up every day,
who stays off the injury list,
who happily signs autographs for kids,
who tries his best day in and day out.
The bar for heroes sure seems
a lot lower these days.

Is Baseball Dying?

Baseball, woven into
the fabric of our lives
is being ripped asunder,
shredded by the violence of football,
and the video game pace of basketball.
Stands emptying, fans aging,
games starting and ending too late,
all the while with the cost of a
family outing devouring a week's wages.
Kids nowadays look for glory
as quarterbacks or point guards,
and nobody ever listens to games
broadcast on the radio anymore.
Once there was a fair chance
that any team could win the pennant,
but now money stalks the batter's box,
and only a few big market teams
can vie for the best players.
With its slow pace, baseball
has dropped the fly ball of its appeal,
and if changes aren't made soon,
the game will drift into a sepia-tinged
memory in the annals of American history.

Karl Spooner—Who?

There are men of my generation
who still argue who was better—
Mantle, Mays, or Snider, but my childhood hero was
Karl Benjamin Spooner.
Who?
He was a young flame-thrower
in his rookie year for the old Brooklyn Dodgers.
I saw him, larger than life, at Ebbets Field,
striking out fifteen Giants in his debut.
His star fell as quickly as it had risen,
a meteoric fastball blazing across the baseball sky.
Now, ensconced deep into my sofa,
deep into my seventh decade,
I doze, nodding silently at the TV,
nodding at the new acolytes
trying to catch the comet of success.
Nobody remembers Karl Spooner anymore.
But I do, acknowledging the power and
the perfidy of the baseball gods
who ordain who shall rise to the heavens,
and who shall fall, ignominiously, into the sea.

Missing Part of My Life During Covid

I miss the crack of the bat,
the slap of a hockey stick,
the whoosh of the net,
the thunder of a tackle.
I miss part of my life.
I do not want
a half of a season,
a third of a season,
a quarter of a season.
I want a full season
where I can watch my teams
fall and climb in the standings,
where play is arranged out
over a full schedule,
where players have time
to grow and develop.
Now I am playing with half a deck,
a third of my interest,
a quarter of my enthusiasm.
Sports are a missing part of my life,
and I feel amputated.

Movie Quotes and Baseball

It's a little-known secret
there exists a great correlation
between famous movie quotes
and baseball. I submit the following:

"We're not in Kansas anymore."
    A Royals road trip
"I coulda been a contender."
    The Mets fail again to make the playoffs
"Go ahead, make my day."
    Hey, batter, you like my 100-mph fastball?
"You talking to me?"
    Ump arguing with player over called third strike
"What we have is a failure to communicate."
    Pitcher and catcher can't agree on signals
"Show me the money."
    Contract negotiations.
"I'm walking here."
    Batter walked on four straight balls
"I want to be alone."
    Reliever giving up walk-off home run
"It's alive, it's alive."
    A rookie pitcher's fastball

Brought to you by me, The Natural, of course!

My Favorite Things

Batters who bat, pitchers who pitch,
New owners who are incredibly rich,
Outfielders whose feet are tied up with wings,
These are a few of my favorite things.

Ace on the mound with a low ERA,
Players who execute a quick double play,
A player who eschews a neck full of bling,
These are a few of my favorite things.

Home run hitter coming to bat,
The lady won't sing, the one who is fat,
Dreams of acquiring a World Series ring,
These are a few of my favorite things.

Hot dog vendors, then there is beer,
A reliever comes in, we loudly cheer,
A pitcher so wily, his ball on a string,
These are a few of my favorite things.

When the fans yell,
When the rafters ring,
When I'm feeling sad,
I simply remember my favorite things,
And then I don't feel so bad.

My First Baseman's Glove

On a cold November night
I started cleaning out an old closet,
looking for my childhood amid the
ancient notebooks, discarded electronics,
and little-worn or remembered clothing.
I finally found the Holy Grail of my youth—
my tattered and treasured first baseman's glove.
With patched leather and loose strings,
and the red Rawlings label,
I clutched it close to my chest,
imagining once more
tricky grounders and scooped-up throws
gently nestling in the lobster claw of my mitt.
Few items in my closet have generated such
tender memories of waiting for the next batter
to hit a screaming liner my way.
I considered placing the glove
on an honored shelf,
but decided instead it was best
to acknowledge my advanced years,
and not dwell or romanticize the past.
I put the glove back in the closet.

Nobody Lives in K.C.

Seriously,
who lives in Kansas City,
stuck somewhere in the middle of the U.S.?
It does not have the panache of
Boston, San Francisco, or New York.
It is not as beautiful as Savannah,
nor as famous as Dallas.
Airplanes fly over it with nary a glance,
and its only claim to fame lies with
the corporation office of Hallmark Cards.
Seriously,
have you ever met anyone from K.C.?
Nevertheless,
when they were in the World Series a while back
I became an unabashed admirer of their small ball.
I roared with the fans at Kauffman Stadium
rooting for the underdog in blue uniforms.
This is my way of standing up for the little guy,
even if they played in some obscure place,
where seriously, nobody lives.

Nobody Remembers Punchball

A clerk at the local sports store
bounces a small, pink "Spaldeen."
He hardly knows what he has in his hands.
He has my childhood in his hands.
Much more than half a century ago,
I, too, bounced a ball from one hand to another.
On the cement playgrounds of Brooklyn,
I tried to stretch a single into a double,
sliding into second base at my own peril,
blood worth the two-bagger.
Afternoons morphed into the end of childhood,
as I prayed for just one more inning.
I should go tell that clerk to be more careful
with my Spaldeen and my memories,
as he is now charged with responsibility
of being the Official Scorer of the
countless games only I can remember.

No Joy in Mudville

It's only a game, you tell yourself,
no loss of eye or limb,
or, God forbid, a family member.
Still, how do you handle loss
by a team you have staked
your season's long hopes on?
"Wait 'til next year," is the old bromide,
but I am running out of years.
This die-hard fan does not wish
to die without a championship.
Million-dollar ballplayers have
failed me, and I take it personally.

The stands are now empty,
the lights have been turned off,
and Mighty Casey has struck out.
The winter wind laughs in my face,
telling me, so much for my dreams.

On Seeing a Brooklyn Dodgers Baseball Cap

It's been many years since
my beloved Brooklyn Dodgers
stole away in the middle of the night
and broke my 13-year-old heart.
Nostalgia swelled when I saw an old man
walking on the avenue with a cane,
sporting the white "B" and blue cap
of my all-time favorite team.
I can still name all the players,
their positions and numbers
as I vividly recall when they won
their one and only World Series.
The Duke, Gil and Pee Wee
stand in the batter's box of my memory:
Robinson is the speed I wish I had then.
Furillo, with his strong right arm.
So, thank you old man with a cane.
Thank you for taking me back
to the field of my childhood dreams.

On Winning

When my team has swept a series,
there is no doubt I feel the joy.
When my team has shut out its opponent,
Why do I refuse to be shut up inside?
When my favorite player goes 4 for 4,
why do I feel I could play in the Bigs?
I control the tides; I ride the waves.
I have a great many things to say
happily to family and friends.
Shouldn't I receive some major credit
for my longtime loyalty?
Shouldn't my years of faithful allegiance
be rewarded by a string of victories?
C'mon guys, belt out a win.
I feel my life is on a winning streak.
I can't wait for the playoffs to begin.

Patsy's Pork Store

Myopic, good field?
—a relative term in Little League ball,
no hit—just stand there, stupid,
a walk is as good as a hit.
I played an irregular first base,
deathly afraid of making an error.
Who in the 6th grade
wants to be ridiculed?
I did not recognize then the
greater embarrassment.
Emblazoned on the back of
my uniform in large red letters
was, "PATSY'S PORK STORE,"
the sponsor of our woebegone team,
a decidedly un-kosher emporium
to be shunned by close family members.
I do not remember my batting average,
but I do remember that sign,
a walking advertisement for a store
I'd never be allowed to enter.

Pitchers and Catchers Report

Pitchers and catchers report in two weeks,
hard to believe when a baseball
would now freeze in mid-air.
Players would not only slide home,
but also, into first, second and third.
And the walk from the bull pen
would be accomplished with a sleigh-ride in.
Managers would call time out
for a break of hot chocolate,
and the lonely right fielder
would have time to build
an individual icehouse on
the snow-covered outfield grass.
But while freezing here up north,
I can comfort myself with the thought
that the cold will soon dissipate,
circulation will return,
and spring will soon emerge,
with the cry of "play ball" enkindling
the summer season of my soul.

Poetry in the Minor Leagues

Sitting on the bench, waiting
hopefully for my turn at bat,
I stare out across the old ball field
at the old manufacturing plant upstate,
just beyond the right field fence.
The factory used to turn out poems,
supplying a living wage to
writers and poets of all ages.
They would have worked for nothing,
enjoying the sunrises and sunsets
over the lazy town river, describing
various colors of the sky's palette.
With paper and pen, they carved out
intricate and masterful work.
But now all writing has been
transferred to the city, pulsing
electronically from place to place,
often without any artistic input at all.
The factory and the ballpark
closed ten years ago,
and my call up to the majors
seems doubtful at best.

Redemption, Baseball's Crowning Glory

So, you blew a 4–3 lead in the 9th.
So, you committed an error in the 8th.
So, you hung a curve in the 7th.
So, what!
Tomorrow Is another day, Scarlett.
You will rise from the ashes of Atlanta.
Listen up, Casey, you struck out
with a very mighty swing.
So, what!
Mudville will always have your back.
Sun and warmth willing,
there is always a game
to be played the next day.
You will have ample opportunities
to win in a variety of ways again.
You can go 0 for 4 one day and
then bounce back 4 for 4 the next.
The beauty of baseball lies
in its forgiveness with the future promise
that tomorrow can and will be better.
Hope is not a thing with feathers,
but a fly ball with a healthy chance
of clearing the fence.

Reply to Replays

Nobody could ever accuse baseball
of being the fastest sport in the world.
Its slow turtle speed harkens back to an age
when carriage horses clip-clopped
on cobblestone roads and lazy barges
floated down the Erie Canal.
Now, a new scourge has afflicted
our treasured American pastime,
allowing baseball to crawl
at an even deadlier pace.
Dreaded challenges and replays
have infected every aspect of the game.
Time outs are called as umpires don headsets
to electronically decide issues on the field.
Both ball and runner seemed to have arrived
at home plate at the same time,
and offices in New York swing into service,
surveying thirty-seven different angles
before rendering a final decision.
Where are the umpires of old,
the ones that had the courage of their convictions?
These men were not afraid to toss a batter
without the aid of some modern hardware.
Get rid of all the machines and gadgets.
Baseball can ill-afford to become even slower.
As a life-long fan, growing older every minute,
I simply just do not have the time.

Requiem for a Losing Ball Club

Rest in peace, my poor, losing club.
You tried your best, but the baseball gods
threw you some wicked curves.
Injuries snapped at the heels of your infielders.
Injuries pulled at the arms of your rotation,
and poor play by all, at different times,
doomed any chance of success.
So, gather up your bats and gloves.
Clean out your lockers and find
your way home to wives and girlfriends.
Take some solace you were granted permission
to play in the highest echelons of the game.
Take courage that life is a continuum,
that losses this year can be converted
into wins the next.
Know that the promise of spring training
makes believers of us all.
Upon the ashes of this season,
we will build a better ball club,
with a few timely player moves, for sure.
Last year's stats will soon be forgotten,
and we will rise again once more
to revel in the green fields of a new day.

Sahr Amara

"I have been in this country for six months.
Yet, I do not understand much
about American teenagers.
They have so much, but little of value.
They even want more; nothing satisfies them.
In West Africa, when I was in primary school,
I had to walk three miles to class, barefooted.
Here I run in shoes that cushion my every step.
In my country if I ate more than once a day
I thanked Allah for his blessings.
Here, they eat for lack of something better to do.
In my country education is a gift, much prized.
Here, it is an arduous task, little respected.
The American teen is open and friendly,
like the morning African sun.
But he is as shallow as the stream
in the road during the rainy season.
I am trying hard to understand American culture.
It will take me more than six months.
It will take me more than six months, also,
to understand their strange game of baseball."

Sandlot Ball

Yes, literally.
Before manicured fields,
before fathers pretending
to be concerned coaches,
before batting helmets, knee braces,
and elbow pads—there was a sandlot,
squished between apartment buildings.
We learned the fundamentals
without benefit of instruction
through trial and error, mostly errors.
We were "The Generals"—
Crayola-emblazoned on our white tee shirts.
Bobby played short, and I, first,
and we played until the ball
disappeared in the gathering darkness.
I still remember my number, 14,
proud of the fact that at nine years old,
I belonged to the community of ball players.
Now as an old man, I sit in front of the TV,
 watch my team and remember.
We were "The Generals."

Scouting Report

"Though he may well be a
promising minor league poet,
probably triple A caliber,
we doubt he is ready for the big show now.
He can certainly field all kinds of topics,
albeit with limited vision, but his poetic swing
demonstrates a lack of bat speed and consistency.
He is rather rigid in his poetic stance,
and is not amenable to changing his grip on
unrhymed free verse of 15–20 lines.
He has not shown the kind of power
necessary to clear the literary fences.
His poetry, while unsuited to
the pastoral demands of the game,
does exhibit urban uniqueness.
What we like best about him is
his gritty tenacity of penning over 3,000 poems.
We wish him well, but at this point we cannot
see offering him a major league contract."

Second Place

Second place has always gotten a bum rap.
Phrases like, "second fiddle," "second banana,"
"also-ran," and "runner-up," to name a few
of the pejorative terms that indicate
you have not garnered the top prize.
But what is so wrong with second place?
It's an accomplishment in and of itself.
It's a cozy nook that fits just behind first place.
There may even be prize money.
In a competitive world, not everybody
 can throw their hands up and take a victory lap.
So have seconds, slide safely into second,
and avoid the glaring spotlight
of celebrity interviews and photo shoots.
I will put on my second-hand shirt,
select my second favorite hat,
and walk slowly down Second Avenue,
shunning the rush of people who
are insanely driven to be first in everything.

Silly Names in Baseball #1

How silly baseball names are.
We root for strange fauna.
We extol inanimate objects.
Do menageries like
Tigers, Cubs and Diamondbacks
step up to the plate?
Do birds like
Orioles, Blue Jays and Cardinals
toss the ball around wing to wing?
Do the Red Sox and the White Sox
play in the same laundry bin?
Other questions arise:
Are Mariners too busy fishing for Marlins?
What have the Dodgers dodged lately?
And how come only tall Giants record strikeouts?
Let's not forget that Brewers may be
too drunk to swing a bat, and Royals too snooty
to get down and dirty on the base paths.
In addition, Padres are too holy to steal signs.
Best to name ball teams after
the cities they represent, like they do
in soccer - Manchester, Leicester, Brighton.
Lastly, who do the Guardians guard?
Let's get rid of these silly names.

Silly Names in Baseball #2

When I was a kid, I was hounded by
a particularly mean moniker, "Four Eyes!"—
due to my incredibly poor vision,
only partially helped by
Coke-bottle sized glasses.
It got me thinking whether ballplayers
enjoy nicknames they've earned.
Walter Johnson might have liked
"Big Train" because his fastball
came roaring through.
Lou Gehrig might have been proud
of his "Iron Horse" because
it denotes longevity and strength.
"Dizzy Dean" might have accepted his flightiness,
and Joe DiMaggio might have enjoyed
an ocean ride on his "Yankee Clipper."
Yet, I would have accepted any nickname—
"Catfish," "Splendid Splinter," "Sultan of Swat,"
anything but the "four eyes" of my youth
while trying to scratch out a single
on the playing fields of Brooklyn.

Sports for the Masses

What about TV sports for normal people?
What about a World Series
for the athletically challenged?
I mean, how many Americans are gifted jocks?
I don't know any major leaguers,
hockey goalies, or hulking linemen.
I can't afford games in major arenas,
and I don't follow the tweets of
high-priced baseball stars.
Perhaps an Olympic style program
could be aired showcasing events like:
- Fastest sprinting to the outlet store
- Most good deeds done in a day
- Most patience on a post office line
- Least time worrying about money

I do not take vitamins or supplements.
I do not spend hours at the gym.
Where is my trophy, my highlight reel,
my blue ribbon for being a regular guy?
I want to see my name on the giant scoreboard,
the one over the center field wall.

Street Games

This is my last nostalgia poem, I swear.
Punchball
There is no use reliving the past.
Stoopball
There are enough things to worry about
Boxball
without dredging up the past.
Hit the Penny
The past is quite dead, you know.
Three-Box Baseball
You can't change what was.
Off-the-Curb
Those days are gone forever.
Chinese Handball
I will never go back to the 2nd Street Park.
You have my word on that.

Surely, He's Worth More

He signed for $426 million.
Surely, he's worth more.
How much is that for each home run?
How much is that per new fan
brought to the ballpark?
I have other questions, too.
How many meals would this
tidy sum buy for the needy?
How many schools can be built?
You will tell me it's what the market will bear,
and I will tell you that no one is worth
$426 million—no entertainer, no politician,
no athlete in any professional sport.
Has our country become so warped
that we can say without flinching,
"He's worth every penny, even more"?
It is clear we have hitched our country's values
to the crack of the bat, the flight of the ball,
going deep, deep over the right field fence.

Teacher All-Star

Several years ago,
on a cool Minnesota night,
the coronation of Jeter had begun.
Idina Menzel sang, "The Star-Spangled Banner,"
and a large American flag draped the field.
Oh, surprise, surprise—my heart jumped.
Major league baseball was going
to honor teachers this very night,
one representative for each of the 30 teams.
It was about time teachers
claimed the national spotlight.
They were all lined up on the field,
in uniforms, waiting to be announced.
Seeing that might inspire some child
in Topeka or Tacoma to become a teacher.
But before the big moment, the cameras
broke away for a commercial.
So much for teachers.
Parents, teach your kids to be ballplayers.
They're so much more important, you know.
They might even get to be on TV.

Ten in a Row

"You can't touch this.
My fastball dances like the wind,
and my slider will eat you up alive.
Look, man, I'm in the zone.
Even a bad call by the ump
don't bother me none.
My change-up is filthy,
and my curve is untouchable.
All my pitches are working great.
Only two pitchers, Nola and Seaver
have struck out ten in a row.
What? You're taking me out?
Are you serious?
My pitch count is too high?
I just struck out ten hitters in a row!
C'mon skipper, one more batter.
I own this guy."

The Almost No-Hitter and the Open Boat

The Toronto pitcher, one batter away
from a no-hitter, peers in for the sign,
so close to perfection, he can taste it.
How many chances, he wonders,
do I get to go down in baseball history?

In another century, in another story,
a boat, foundering in the waters
off the rugged coastline, fights for survival.
"Why, oh God, do you tease me?" asks the sailor.

The batter sees the pitch, as large as a balloon,
and slaps a hard single to right ruining the no-hitter.
"Why, oh God, did you tease me?" asks the pitcher.

There is always hope for the next game, the next trip,
but why must the universe be so cruel
in offering gifts of life and immortality,
only to pull them back with benign vengeance?

The Antidote to Aging

As I grow old, with various body parts
abandoning me in droves,
or conditions torturing
my physical well-being,
happily, I think upon baseball,
where the sun shines on the field,
and Ernie Banks says, "Let's play two."
What keeps me younger?
A five-year-old in the stands
with an oversized glove
knowing he will catch a foul ball.
A rookie up from Triple A
stepping into the batter's box
for his first at bat.
A teenager at the ballpark
learning from his father
how to fill out a scorecard.
I don't go to many games now.
I am slower than a walk to first base,
but when I hear the umpire cry,
"Play ball," I know that despite
uninvited encroachments upon my body,
the world still holds a nine-inning
cornucopia of future and joyful possibilities.

The Batting Cage

Long ago, in the arcades of Coney Island,
the batting cages beckoned.
You dropped in your quarters,
selected your speed,
and dreamed for the moment
you were a major leaguer
swinging for the fences.
The bat was too heavy, the pitches too fast,
and you flailed with tepid swings,
trying to make contact
with the ball that zipped by
before you even saw it.
Now, in the later innings of my life,
the cage exists as metaphor for
missed chances and opportunities,
with wild swings hitting nothing but air.
What I would like is another turn at bat,
one where the sun is always shining,
and the bat feels right in my hands.
I am twelve again,
ready to step up to the plate,
confident this time I'm about to hit
the ball right out of the park.

The Body Shambles

If I can sue my knees for non-support,
I can bring charges against
my heart, my eyes, my stomach.
Years ago, my internal organs
purred along in working and efficient order,
and except for occasional illness,
I pretty much took my health for granted,
the symphony of all parts working in sync.
Now, when I wake up,
I do an informal roll call,
listening to various areas
who wish to request a sick day.
Doctors assure me I'm still good,
even to play softball,
but I do wonder how long
my internal clock will continue to run.
I do not fear mortality,
just incapacity.
I wish for all my interior structures
to message me and say,
"You're in the clear, pal, at least for a few
more years. You can get out your old glove."

The Closer

Who among us is perfect?
Nobody, but we expect
the closer to be, to exhibit skills
far beyond those of mortal man.
Did he blow another save?
Trade him.
Did he blow two saves in a row?
Send him down to Triple A.
His imperfections are our own.
Maybe because our own lives
are far from perfect, we expect
more from the closer than from
anyone else on the team.
Let's value him in story and song,
for he walks the wire, balancing
precariously between wins and losses.
Here is a rousing ovation for the closer.
He has to be the best of us.

The Jewish Ballplayer

Of course, he never plays on
Friday nights or Saturday afternoons.
It's in his contract, and for sure,
like Sandy Koufax, he never suits up
on the High Holidays.
Between innings, he can be seen
reading a book or placing a call
to his mother in New Jersey,
who constantly worries about him, worries
that some *shiksa* goddess will ensnare him,
even though he is a boy still, 28,
playing a boy's game.
He avoids Mickey D's and Taco Bell;
instead, he has his kosher food
delivered to him. His teammates love pastrami.
When he strikes out, he can be heard
murmuring, "Oy!"
But when he blasts a home run,
he exults with a cry of "Halevi"
as he circles the bases,
his *yarmulke* flying.
He proudly wears #18 *(chai),* (life),
and is grateful he, the little *pisher,*
is fortunate enough to play with *chutzpah,*
The Great American Game.

The Losing Pitcher Talks to His Therapist

"Doc, I think I made a breakthrough.
You made me realize that life is more than
pitches thrown, wins and losses.
You supported me in the good times,
when my fastball clipped the corners,
and my curve tied baters up in knots.
You stood by me in the bad times,
when I suffered from performance anxiety
on the mound and in the bedroom.
You made me see I needed the cheers
to validate and enhance my ego,
that I had to have the love of the fans
because my mother constantly criticized me,
and my father showed little warmth.
You opened my eyes to the fact
my anger at the opposing team was only
lashing out, anger displacement.
You explained my folly of associating
my self-worth with my earned run average.
I am eternally grateful to you,
but I do have a small favor to ask -
Can I see you for an emergency session?
We have an important series coming up."

The Mets Meet the Met

Wife to husband:
You'll love *La Traviata*.
The opera is lyrical.
Keep your eyes on the main stars.
It's a story of love.
Violetta is in love with Alfredo,
but the course of true love
never runs smooth.
It's the best production I have seen in a while.

Husband to wife:
You'll love the Mets
The stadium is electric.
Keep your eyes on the main stars.
You gotta love this team.
Alonzo is batting below .300,
but he will get better, I'm sure.
The baseball gods believe in redemption.
It's the best team I have seen in a while.

She: Will this game ever be over?
He: The singer took too long to die.

The Natural

I am swinging for the fences
in the Class A poetry League.
Like Roy Hobbs,
I have dropped out of
the major leagues of writing,
and now after ten years away,
I must pack my "Wonder Pen"
to start all the way at the bottom.
The wait at the plate seems interminable—
"We'll let you know if it's a hit
six months from now, and then allow you
to run the bases, if published, in a year or so."
Do I have that much time?
I size up each opposing magazine manager
to see what pitches he will call for:
The sensuous curve of a sweet lyric?
The sizzling fastball of blank verse?
The slow change of a long prose poem?
I brace myself for the inevitable "No."
I must try to spray my writing
to as many fields as possible,
left, center and right, and maybe one day
I will hit the high arc of a towering poem
and bust out all the lights again.

They Don't Know Punchball

When the national TV baseball announcers
met the word, "punchball," they didn't
even know what it was, thereby denigrating
and obliterating my whole childhood.
It's obvious they never lived in New York.
"Do you punch a baseball with
your hands?" they asked.
"No, that would break your hand." Duh.
"What about with a soccer or kickball?"
"No, I don't think that's it."
They looked it up.
"It's like baseball," they said.
"You toss it up to yourself,
and punch the ball."
How could these guys be so ignorant about
the game that defined my young life?
How could they not know I played
punchball every day in the Second Street Park?
Punchball, with a bright, pink
"Spaldeen" tucked into my back pocket.
You can keep your national broadcasters.
Just let me go back to my park and
try to hit one over the tall wire fence.

Time on Their Hands

Baseball exists as one of the few sports
not ruled by the tyranny of the clock.
It rolls across the American landscape
with a pastoral slowness, unencumbered
by the demands of ticking minutes, without
the noise of buzzers, horns, and whistles.
This may be a good thing as players in the field
standing as frozen as toy soldiers can now
contemplate the meaning of the universe.
In the lull of games, they can dwell upon
their relationship to God, their purpose,
and other cosmic matters usually reserved
for philosophers and theologians.
Such idle time could be spent
pursuing ideas that are literally far afield.
The game then would be better served
by bringing to the majors, thoughtful young men
who have more on their minds than
the location of the next fly ball coming their way.

Unwatchable

What do you do when your team
becomes unwatchable,
when you suffer too many errors,
too many blown saves, too few hits?
Do you give up your cable subscription,
berate the players for incompetence,
criticize the manager for wrong decisions?
Or, do you take the philosophical stance,
placing your hopes in a September call-up?
No, long ago, you took a vow of loyalty.
You said, "I do" to the marriage
of you and your team, and as with
the important relationships in your life,
you are duty-bound to honor your commitment,
honor it "in sickness and in health."
Unwatchable as your team may be,
as sickly and wan as an orphan,
you are tethered with ties
as strong as any in your life.
They are simply your team.

Walk-Off Home Run

There's nothing more definitive
than the home team's announcer's call,
"Walk-off home run! Walk-off home run!" -
assuredly not as famous as Russ Hodges'
"The Giants win the pennant!
The Giants win the pennant,"
but thrilling nonetheless.
In a world of shifting morality,
and less-than-certain answers,
it is particularly satisfying to see
that the suddenness of such a call
decides the outcome once and for all.
One knows then, with striking clarity,
who has won, who has lost,
that it makes it easier to face
an unsettling and problematic world.
Let me know where I stand.
Do not confuse me with muddled maybes
and puzzling half-truths.
Let me stand in the batter's box
with the score tied in the 9th,
and let me decide with one mighty swing
and my own skill whether
I've won or lost the game.

We Need Our Heroes

Because we lead insignificant lives,
because time has thrown us into
a maelstrom of stress and anxiety,
because our reality bears
little resemblance to our dreams,
we need our heroes front and center.
A rookie's towering blast,
a pitcher's string of zeroes,
a third baseman's spear of a line drive—
all heroic feats that enable us to soar
above our own day-to-day groundhog days.
The commuter slog,
the demanding boss,
the annoying in-law—
wait, give me the sports pages
so I can mingle with my idols,
and pretend for an afternoon
that my own life
has some grains of grandeur, linking
me to a level I can only aspire to reach.

When My Team Wins

A rainbow morning,
a winning lottery ticket,
a visit from an old friend—
such are the small delights
when the baseball gods
ordain a winning streak.
Then there is little I can't do.
There is little they can't do.
I am thrilled to see the world
through baseball-covered glasses.
I round the bases of my job.
I throw a no-hitter into the proposal
that I pitch to my boss.
I luxuriate in the bright sunshine
that floods the outfield grass.
But I know nothing is forever,
especially win streaks,
so I prize these glory days
until the time they are taken away,
and my team drifts back
to its old familiar ways.

White Man's Baseball

According to comedian Chris Rock,
basketball and football are "cool,"
and baseball decidedly is not.
Which raises the question, is baseball
a sport principally watched
by old white men huddled over their TVs?
Baseball is old-fashioned, he argues,
and has as much buzz as the field it's played on.
May I suggest that he, and the sports
he champions, are too fast, too frenetic,
governed by a clock to the exact second.
I have little to do with acrobatic dunks,
and thundering tackles that are
physically impossible for me.
I am perfectly comfortable with the
leisurely pace of nine innings.
Baseball may be uncool for the cool life,
but I vote with my remote,
or occasionally I buy a ticket
for the slow, unhurried dance
that is the game I love.

Wild Card

Imagine your whole professional life
decided in one single second.
Imagine your recent hard-won efforts
rendered a success or failure
by a single supervisor's sentence.
How cruel the world must seem
if futures are based
on a single flip of a coin,
a single roll of the dice,
a chance encounter, a misstep off a curb,
a scratch of a lottery ticket—
all individual haphazard events.
There's more—the wrong turn at the fork,
the sudden hamstring pull,
the loss of a race by a hundredth of a second.
Are we just the product of happenstance,
fortunes determined by the vagaries of a single second?
Life, not as a collective accumulation of work,
but made up of irrevocable starburst moments.
Is this fair in life, or in baseball?
Shouldn't we at least play two out of three?

Winter Ball

News flash!
Baseball owners have decided
To extend the season
well into the winter months.
They say they need more money.
Of course, some changes
need to me made. To wit:

*Orange baseballs will now be used
to contrast with the whiteness of the snow.
*Potential grounders, stuck in the snow,
will now be counted as strikes.
*Only line drives and fly balls
will be considered hits.
*Pitchers will be allowed to wear
gloves on both hands.
*Snow shoes will be worn
instead of cleats.
*If there is frostbite,
The game shall be called.
*Fans will be given hand-warmers
and free hot chocolate.

Winter ball will be successful, owners claim.
"We need more games to satisfy fan hunger
for the American pastime," they say.
"Everybody should be happy now."

Ending Poems

The Last Picture Show

It's early October now,
and for most of the teams in the majors
the big screen above center field
has been turned off.
The seats in the theater of baseball
lie empty with ticket takers and concessionaires
exiting quickly as the last show of the season
ends with a weak grounder to third,
and an easy toss to first.
Final credits roll on the scoreboard as
the old manager buttons up his windbreaker.
In his mind he edits the highlights
and lowlights of the 162 presentations this year,
some shows a comedy, others a drama.
He doubts whether he will be rehired next year.
He looks out towards the now darkened
scoreboard screen, perhaps for the last time,
doffs his cap in genuine gratitude for the game,
and walks slowly into the coming winter.
The great stadium sits alone and bare,
a silent movie house now.

Why We Cheer

Why are we so passionate
about a sport or team
we really have no connection to?
Is it part of our desire to be connected to
something larger than ourselves?
We are neither owner nor player,
just some poor fan who will pay
an exorbitant amount of money
to sit in the second deck.
We have no official stake,
are not related to any of the players,
and have no say in whatever
quirky direction the ball or team will take.
So, why the cheers and jeers?
Our tribal passions are on full display,
full-throated, sure, but one-sided.
The team does not care that much about us.
It's passion without reciprocity;
It's intensity without intimacy, safe.
Nothing is required of us, save our loyalty.
We have fallen under the spell
of the oldest love story in history—
unrequited love which we pay for!
We wait yearly to have our hearts broken.
But, in the end, we need to be in love,
even if that love flows mainly in just one direction.

Why Baseball Is Important

On the constant cusp of political discord,
when the country splits between
Democratic and Republican entreaties,
when there seems to be more
division, sorrow, and enmity
than we think we can stand,
we need the regularity of normalcy,
that baseball has always provided,
the choreography of catches,
the balance of hit and pitch,
the familiarity of the fans' roar.
We need the comfort of old statistics,
the veneration of our heroes,
the link to our childhoods,
when the only thing that mattered
was the ability to hit the ball squarely.
We need baseball, and its long traditions
to remind ourselves of who we are—
good people proving the old values,
enjoying an afternoon contest,
confident the game will not end in a brawl.

About the Author

Mel Glenn is the author of 12 books for young adults, including *Jump Ball, Split Image,* and *Who Killed Mr. Chippendale?* which was nominated for the Edgar Allen Poe Mystery Award.

Mel retired from the New York City public school system in 2001, after teaching 34 years of high school English. He now devotes his time to reading, writing, and speaking across the country in conferences and schools.

He lives in Brooklyn, with his wife Elyse, a retired elementary school teacher. His son Jonathan works at a national news organization, and his son Andrew works in engineering for a financial tech company.

In early 2023, Mel was thrilled to meet his first grandchild, Casey.

Mel Glenn's website is:
melglenn.com.

www.ingramcontent.com/pod-product-compliance
Lightning Source LLC
Chambersburg PA
CBHW070938160426
43193CB00011B/1727